Caravaggio

By John Gash

RIZZOLI ART SERIES

Series Editor: Norma Broude

Caravaggio

(1571–1610)

THE TWENTIETH century has seen a great upswing of interest in Italian baroque art. But of all the seventeenth-century Italian painters to have emerged with enhanced stature from this scrutiny, Caravaggio alone has become a household name. This is partly due to his promotion by art historians, who have been less inclined than their predecessors to damn him with faint praise as an important exponent of naturalism whose vision was nonetheless circumscribed by the strangeness of his personality. Indeed, he is now often placed on a par with his previously more renowned Netherlandish contemporaries, Rubens and Rembrandt, both of whom he influenced.

Yet this virtual apotheosis has not been unconnected with a wider, peculiarly twentieth-century perception of his "alienated" character and its impact on his art. Whereas Rembrandt and Rubens have always been admired for the depth and range of their humanity, Caravaggio now often appeals by virtue of what once repelled: his reputation as an enfant terrible. His capricious nature, aggressive behavior, and bohemian way of life have intrigued the modern imagination—fueling the notion of him as an embattled outsider who channeled the complexities of his own makeup into an assertively iconoclastic art.

One of the more striking manifestations of this new mythology has been the wealth of fiction his life has inspired—culminating in Derek Jarman's fine film, *Caravaggio* (1986). The particular aspect of Caravaggio's non-conformism that Jarman and others have sought to project is his homosexuality, with the result that he has become something of an icon for the gay community. Although the documentary record implies that Caravaggio was bisexual, the testimony of the paintings strongly suggests a predominantly homosexual orientation. In fact, in the early half-lengths of scantily clad youths with still-life accessories of flowers or fruit (see *The Lute Player*, plate 3; and *Bacchus*, fig. 1), as well as in the subsequent scurrilous burlesques on the high-flown poetry of Michelangelo's Sistine Chapel *ignudi* (see *Victorious Cupid*, plate 10), a homosexual agenda seems clearly enough to coexist with the naturalistic one. In a recent interview, Jarman went one stage further, arguing that the "extremity" of *David with the Head of Goliath* (plate 15) is indicative of Caravaggio's homosexual sensibility.[1] Whatever its origins, the extremism that characterized Caravaggio's recorded actions had a decisive effect on his work, bringing a cutting edge to his polemical revival of naturalism in art. Of the major European painters who have sought to overturn established artistic orthodoxies through a return to, or strengthening of, naturalism (Courbet, Giotto, Leonardo, Manet, Masaccio), he has some claim to be considered the most revolutionary.

Trained in Milan in the naturalistic modes of Lombardy and Venice, Caravaggio shares the honors with his Bolognese contemporary, Annibale Carracci, for having imaginatively transposed the sixteenth-century north Italian taste for the natural to Rome during the 1590s, thereby dealing a deathblow to the highly artificial and already moribund central Italian style of Mannerism. The two artists' preference for the realistic representation of figures in space and the clear articulation of narrative was in marked contrast to the Mannerist concern with stylized poses, decorative surface pattern, and obliquely conveyed sentiment. But whereas Caravaggio's and Carracci's vigorous new formulations jointly laid the foundations of the baroque, there were notable differences of emphasis between them. Carracci aimed to restore and deepen the tradition of idealized naturalism enshrined in antique sculpture and the art of the High Renaissance masters (especially Raphael) and to reinvoke the pivotal role Raphael had established for preparatory drawings as a means of mediating between observation of the world and artistic construction. Caravaggio insisted on a bolder and more dramatic break. His belief in the overriding importance of imitating nature inspired perhaps his most radical innovation: painting directly from posed models, seemingly without preparatory drawings and with relatively little modification of appearance. Even his famed, and distinctly contrived, system of lighting using strong contrasts of light and shade (chiaroscuro), which he manipulated to powerful dramatic and symbolic effect, has a crucial naturalistic function. For, as Leonardo had recognized, strong light directed into a murky space from above has the effect of enhancing the three-dimensionality of forms. Like a master film director, Caravaggio was prepared to resort to calculated engineering (of lighting and pose) in order to better evoke real presence.

1. *Bacchus.* c. 1597. Oil on canvas, 37½ x 33½". Uffizi, Florence

Michelangelo Merisi was born in the autumn of 1571 in Lombardy, either in Milan or in the fortress town of Caravaggio (after which he was to be called), twenty miles to its east. His father, Fermo Merisi, was architect and majordomo to

Francesco Sforza, Marquis of Caravaggio. Michelangelo trained in Milan under Simone Peterzano, a moderately talented pupil of Titian, from 1584 to about 1588, before moving to Rome, probably in the summer of 1592. None of Caravaggio's pictures from his youth in Lombardy has survived, but one source, intriguingly, claims that he early on became a specialist in portraiture, perhaps thus initiating his obsession with working directly from the model.

The striking originality of Caravaggio's art renders assessment of his artistic influences difficult. His belief in the primacy of imitating nature put a low premium on emulating the styles of even his most illustrious predecessors. Yet it is clear from numerous small individual points of analogy that he was extremely well versed in the various naturalistic traditions of sixteenth-century northern Italy— from the passion for detail and light effects of the Brescian masters Savoldo, Romanino, Moretto, and Moroni, through the Venetian colorism of Titian and Lotto, to the chiaroscuro of Leonardo and his Milanese followers.

In Rome, Caravaggio first did jobbing work for a succession of painter-dealers who were stepping up production to meet the needs of an expanding art market—from the mediocre Lorenzo Siciliano and the accomplished Sienese Antiveduto Grammatica (for both of whom he allegedly did half-lengths) to the most popular young painter in Rome, the late Mannerist Giuseppe Cesari, known as the Cavaliere d'Arpino, for whom he is said to have painted fruits and flowers. This probably means he was painting independent still lifes, a new genre, the reasons for whose emergence about this time are poorly understood. Although Caravaggio's only securely attributed still life, the beautiful *Basket of Fruit*, came later (c. 1598–1601), the distinguished Italian connoisseur Federico Zeri has pinpointed a handful of potential candidates for this embryonic stage of Caravaggio's naturalism.[2]

On the other hand, Caravaggio almost certainly painted for d'Arpino, about 1594–1595, three half-length pictures of youths that feature prominent still lifes of fruit: the so-called *Sick Little Bacchus*, done from his own likeness, *Fruit Vendor*, and a lost *Boy Peeling Fruit*, known through copies. Their appearance could provide a clue to the kind of work Caravaggio had previously executed for Lorenzo and Grammatica.

On leaving d'Arpino's studio, Caravaggio's growing reputation led him to produce religious works for private, probably ecclesiastical, patrons (plate 1) and a new kind of half-length (picturesque narrative genre scenes of more than one figure—e.g., *The Cardsharps*, plate 2), which he may have sold through the fashionable art dealer Maestro Valentino. Indeed, it could have been through Valentino that Caravaggio came into contact with two highly cultivated late-Renaissance polymaths, Cardinal Francesco del Monte and the Marchese Vincenzo Giustiniani, who were destined to become his most important patrons.

These two sophisticated patrons with a taste for aesthetic novelty were attracted by the unprecedented directness of Caravaggio's naturalism. But they also perceptively discerned the adaptability of his style to their own interest in musical subjects and allegory, as in del Monte's *Concert of Youths* (c. 1595–1597), and Giustiniani's *The Lute Player* (plate 3)[3] and *Victorious Cupid* (plate 10).

The precise implication of the symbolism (if any) in *The Lute Player* has been lost to us, although the effeminate youth is singing an identifiable madrigal ("You Know that I Love You"). Yet the painting is cast in the same mold as the previous half-lengths for d'Arpino and, like them, is first and foremost a demonstration piece, designed to show off Caravaggio's skill at representing both the human figure and naturalistic still life. But equally, as with them, its true meaning is lodged in its visual formulation. For whether or not there was any intended symbolism to the choice of subject in these works, their communicative charge lies in the poetic chords that Caravaggio created between the boys and their inanimate equivalents, as in the soaringly elegant flower arrangement of *The Lute Player*, which pointedly parallels the delicate features and curly hair of the lutenist. Such linkages assert the inherently transient nature of beauty and pleasure and underline the variously inflected eroticism of the images.

But one should keep that eroticism in perspective: The fact that nearly all of these boys wear either loose shirts with plunging necklines or pseudo-antique off-the-shoulder garments obviously forms part of the pictures' intended charm. However, their mood varies considerably, from the quiet lyricism of the *Boy Peeling Fruit* to the blatant but ironical propositioning of a second *Bacchus* (fig. 1), probably commissioned about 1597 as a gift from Cardinal del Monte to his protector, Ferdinando I de' Medici. Even *The Lute Player* is no obvious pin-up. It is, in fact, possible that the youth's exotic appearance reflects the actual dress and deportment of a contemporary musician aiming to frame the elegance of his performance with a comparable visual allure.

One detail in the painting would especially seem to point in this direction—the graceful and artificial placement of the left hand follows precisely a prescription in Vincenzo Capirola's Lute Book of 1515–1520: "The left (hand) should use the thumb, as it is more beautiful to see it on the neck (of the instrument)."[4] With Caravaggio it is always difficult to demarcate the realist agenda from the iconographical one.

The half-lengths are indeed finely tuned pieces of observation—painted from posed models and objects placed in the studio, and geared to the maximum evocation of presence. Nothing that will enhance verisimilitude is ignored, from keenly observed details, which run contrary to the generalizing conventions of Renaissance art (maggot-holes in an apple, fig. 1; an excessive length of gut string crinkling out of the peg-box of a lute), to the strategic foregrounding of objects and the play of shadows. And Caravaggio often seeks to cap this sense of actuality with the added dimension of sound—foreshadowing in the parted lips of the *Fruit Vendor* and *The Lute Player* the recurrent motif of an open mouth in his mature art.

Caravaggio also introduces in such works as *The Lute Player* another feature that was to become central to his subsequent religious art—a diagonal shaft of light that slants across the back wall. It is primarily a product of his studio-based naturalism, the source of light by implication a high window in the room in which he has painted his model(s). Yet it simultaneously assumes other functions, both pictorial and expressive: not only does it animate the monotony of the back wall but also serves to emphasize a dramatic moment. From such beginnings, Caravaggio proved adept in the 1590s at evolving idioms suitable for scenes of more than one figure and for religious paintings.

His most significant advance in articulating the interaction of figures occurs in *The Cardsharps*, in which he expanded the early formula of a single figure seated behind a table into a group seated around one. He would continue to use a table as the center of gravity of several of his compositions in ensuing years (see fig. 3 and plates 4, 8, 14). Even when not iconographically essential, it was a useful means of gathering together models and still-life accessories to paint from, and of focusing a dramatic encounter.

The fact that Caravaggio painted directly from the model is attested to both by his seventeenth-century commentators and by the pictures themselves. The former deplored the fact—correctly perceiving its fundamentally subversive nature. For a faithfully reproduced model is not necessarily an apt characterization. And although we remain uncertain to what extent sixteenth-century Venetian painters pioneered the practice, they do not appear to have pursued it with such uncompromising rigor as Caravaggio did. Caravaggio's apparently all but total rejection of the use of preparatory drawing was equally unprecedented and similarly directed at asserting the primacy of the seen over the imagined. Indeed, a spate of recent technical investigations shows that he sometimes fixed the position of the models on the canvas with a few deft, strategically placed incisions using a sharp implement and then proceeded to establish the full contours of the figures with an immaculate brush-drawing technique.[5]

2. *St. Catherine of Alexandria*. c. 1597–1598. Oil on canvas, 68 x 52⅓". Thyssen-Bornemisza Collection, Lugano-Castagnola, Switzerland

It is evident that Caravaggio more than once used the same model for different personages—as, conspicuously, with the girl employed both for *St. Catherine of Alexandria* (fig. 2), done for del Monte about 1597–1598, and for the somewhat later *Conversion of the Magdalen* (fig. 3). It is even possible that he retained a deformity to a finger of the woman's left hand in both works. Such polemical flourishes are consistent with his broader aesthetic. As he told the judge who tried him in 1603 for writing libelous satirical verses about the painter Baglione, a good painter is "one who knows how to paint and imitate natural things well."

This ideology is further reflected in the fact that he never developed a recyclable type for a particular religious person-

3. *The Conversion of the Magdalen*. c. 1597–1599. Oil and tempera on canvas, 39⅓ x 53". Detroit Institute of Arts. Gift of the Kresge Foundation and Mrs. Edsel B. Ford

age. On the contrary—not only did Caravaggio sometimes use the same model for different characters, but he nearly always used a different one for the same character. No two Christs by him are remotely similar (see plates 4, 8, 11, 12).

The elevation of such strategies into a coherent language of religious expression occurred in the second half of the 1590s, as a result of Caravaggio's growing alertness to the emotive properties of light. Light conditions observed in the studio were selectively manipulated in order to register the presence of the divine and emphasize that of the human protagonists. Above all, the motif of a beam of light slanting across a back wall acquired, in a work such as *The Penitent Magdalen* (c. 1596), a specifically religious connotation—as the light of divine grace penetrating the murky desolation of human affairs. It was to become one of his favorite metaphors (see plates 4, 8, 9).

But the clinching impulse toward the fully intensified chiaroscuro of his mature manner may have come from an accident of iconography. For Caravaggio was apparently commissioned during the second half of the 1590s to paint two scenes whose subject is set at night: the small, freely brushed cabinet picture of *The Ecstasy of St. Francis*, for Cardinal del Monte, and *Judith Beheading Holofernes*. The challenge of night scenes stimulated him to a still further reduction of the range of colors that had distinguished his Veneto-Lombard early palette in favor of a bolder conception in which light and shade dominate over color.

The *Judith* in particular has all the hallmarks of Caravaggio's maturity, combining as it does an evocative chiaroscuro with marked foreshortenings and a conspicuous flair for the articulation of dramatic narrative. Its bold contrasts may even have been achieved by Caravaggio painting by lamplight in order to emulate the effect of torchlight in Holofernes's tent. If the picture was painted before the summer of 1599, as most commentators think, it would be the first statement of his definitive style. If not, then the two large canvases of *The Calling* and *Martyrdom of St. Matthew* (plates 4 and 5), which he executed between 23 July 1599 and 4 July 1600 for the side walls of the Contarelli Chapel in San Luigi dei Francési (his first public commission), are all the more revolutionary. Together with two smaller works, *The Crucifixion of St. Peter* and *The Conversion of St. Paul* (plates 6 and 7), done in 1601 for the Cerasi Chapel of Santa Maria del Popolo, they virtually established his reputation overnight as the most persuasive living artistic interpreter of the sacred.

The secret of his success lay in a novel combination: realistic figure-types allied to strong chiaroscuro. The former flattered the aspirations of the Church of the Counter Reformation by emphasizing the common humanity of the saints; the latter pressed home the message by evoking the mystery of the faith.

The two St. Matthew narratives appear to relate to two kinds of studio lighting used by Caravaggio in the following years—sunlight from a high, side window, as seen in *The Calling*, and illumination in a dark room from a lamp placed high above the models, which may have been employed for *The Martyrdom*. The latter would have had the advantage over natural light of providing a constant source of illumination. But he probably continued to use both procedures, sometimes within a single painting.

Caravaggio's variously contrived strategies for an assertive realism would not, however, have been sufficient to ensure such remarkable images were it not for his intuitive grasp of dramatic form. In *The Calling*, the main source of illumination is high up on the right, in *The Martyrdom* on the left. This corresponds to the direction of the action in both pictures, with the light intended to mimic the daylight entering the chapel from a lunette window above the altar. In *The Calling* the light sweeps across the wall past the figures of Christ and his companion, who have just entered the countinghouse, as if a superior force directing their endeavors, its slant paralleling Christ's gathering gesture as he summons the tax collector Levi (Matthew) to the discipleship.

At the same time, Caravaggio was skillful in his positioning of scatterings of light to indicate individual responses. Indeed, he uses light as much to convey human alarm at the workings of providence as the nature of the Godhead itself. It is only one of many examples of dramatic irony in his art. Another is the way in which Caravaggio has cast Matthew's slayer in *The Martyrdom* as one of the nude figures he has been baptizing—suddenly risen up from the font to transform a tranquil scene into one of sound and fury.

This dramatic flair, which would often override the finer points of iconography without subverting the central significance of a narrative, extended on occasion to the inclusion of his self-portrait in religious pictures. In *The Martyrdom* this takes the form of a conceit: Caravaggio as one of the fleeing crowd looks back over his shoulder to witness the holy mystery and his own mastery in re-creating it.

The Contarelli laterals are great pieces of theater, paralleling the pyrotechnics of the Elizabethan-Jacobean stage and heralding the theatricality of baroque art. Their consummate illusion is of sacred events taking place in the space of the chapel. It is an impression that is heightened, here as elsewhere, by Caravaggio's eloquent deployment of both modern and biblical costume.

In *The Crucifixion of St. Peter* and *The Conversion of St. Paul*, there is even greater economy of dramatic means and a more insistent foregrounding of the figures. The pattern of chiaroscuro and quality of light in both works suggest that Caravaggio used a hanging lamp for illumination, as the main figures are picked out in a centralized pool of light. Here Caravaggio compactly directs his resources toward involving the viewer in the drama—with Peter turning on his cross to address the crowd/onlooker, and Saul's arms thrown back in rapture against the picture plane, embracing the light of conversion virtually from the spectator's point of view. Later Caravaggio would alternate between such decontextualizing background darkness and minimal hints of an architectural or landscape setting, shrouded in shadow. With either method, he effectively abolished distinctions of time and place and freed his spotlit figures to loom forward into the spectator's space and consciousness. It does not matter whether the scene is actually meant to be set at night (as it only occasionally is): the darkness in his pictures is St. John of the Cross's "dark night of the soul."

Caravaggio may have intensified his illusionism in the Cerasi Chapel because he was working jointly on the chapel's decoration with Annibale Carracci, who had been commissioned to do the altarpiece of *The Assumption*. These two leading exponents of naturalism took the opportunity of the encounter to assert their respective approaches—with Carracci pushing his fondness for Raphael-esque idealization, even lighting, and coloristic delicacy to a new pitch, and Caravaggio countering with his vigorous anticlassicism. In fact, Caravaggio's formulations have a distinctly polemical edge to them: the backside and muddy feet of Peter's executioner are thrust ostentatiously against the picture plane, and the rump of Paul's horse (a tired Roman dray horse on a hot day) is unceremoniously directed at Carracci's altarpiece.

Such boldness is the more surprising given that Caravaggio's pictures were probably replacements for two others by him that the patron had found unsatisfactory. Comparable disapproval and rejection of his public commissions was to dog his remaining Roman career, despite the fact that patrons continued to vie for his services. Of the five altarpieces that he delivered between 1602 and 1606, one was turned down flat and two (including *The Death of the Virgin*, plate 9) were soon removed. Only *The Entombment of Christ* (plate 11) and *The Madonna of Loreto* prospered, both of them to become highly popular devotional images.

The reason for the rejection of certain pictures was their perceived lack of decorum: that is, sacred figures were represented with insufficient dignity. Sometimes it is easy to see how Caravaggio's ostentatious rhetoric of the real offended. For example, in an altarpiece of *St. Matthew and the Angel*, done in 1602 to crown his achievement in the Contarelli Chapel, he foreshortened the bare foot of the gormless-looking apostle immediately above the center of the altar.

When he found himself thwarted by censure of his public commissions, Caravaggio was able to pursue his experiments in works for sympathetic private collectors. For Giustiniani he painted a scurrilous Cupid (plate 10); and for Ciriaco Mattei, *The Supper at Emmaus* (plate 8), which seems devised above all to demonstrate his skills at foreshortening and still-life painting.

Yet it would be wrong to view Caravaggio's program as exclusively stylistic. For despite his cavalier attitude to the finer points of iconography (as in *The Supper*, where one might question the presence of a basket of fruit seasonal to the autumn of 1601 when the picture was painted, but not to Easter, when the episode portrayed is meant to have occurred), he is always conscious of the need to focus a narrative through some striking piece of theater. In *The Supper*, the double arm span of the apostle on the right, which could be seen simply as a gratuitous illusionistic flourish, equally serves as the man's bewildered assertion that he had last seen Christ, with whom he is now confronted, dead on the cross.

Caravaggio's taste for investing plausible gestures with

symbolic connotations was significantly refined during the ensuing years, as can be seen in *The Entombment* (plate 11) and *The Raising of Lazarus* (plate 12). In the former, the outstretched arms of the Virgin (center) double as a protective, embracing gesture and an allusion to the Crucifixion; whereas the raised arms of Mary Cleophas (top right) incorporate a climax to the mourners' grief and hint at Christ's future resurrection.

This mimetic symbolism was part of the fundamentally theatrical approach to art that made Caravaggio such a compelling exponent of Christian doctrine (despite lapses of decorum) and the prime instigator of the baroque. But the particular cast of his ritualistic mime has more in common with our own theater. In this, as in other aspects of his art (his decontextualizing chiaroscuro; the alienated quality that he brings to the rendition of violent action, both of which inspired the playwright Samuel Beckett)—he is at heart a modern.

Just as prophetic of our sense of a fragmented reality are the many contradictions inherent in Caravaggio's art between naturalistic ambition, sensual interest, and religious expression. They lie at the heart of a creative energy that was fueled by psychic tension. The internal conflicts that led del Monte to characterize him as "very strange" escalated considerably during his maturity, issuing in a succession of violent acts. Between October 1600 and September 1605 he was arraigned no less than eleven times before the courts for offenses ranging from libel, to armed assault (three times), to throwing stones at the window of his ex-landlady and a plate of artichokes at a waiter. The saga culminated on 29 May 1606, when he killed an acquaintance, Ranuccio Tommasoni, in a brawl over a disputed bet on a game of tennis. That incident forced Caravaggio to flee Rome under the threat of capital punishment, and he spent the last four years of his life in the south. He progressed first to Naples; then to Malta, where he was made a Knight of St. John, only to be imprisoned for insulting a senior member of the Order; next (after escaping, but with the Knights at his heels) to the Sicilian cities of Syracuse, Messina, and Palermo, leaving in his wake a trail of major altarpieces; before returning to Naples (where he was badly wounded in a fight that may have involved the Knights); and finally, by boat north to Porto Ercole on the Tuscan coast, where he died on 18 July 1610.

Caravaggio's art saw three significant shifts of emphasis in the last years, all to some degree conditioned by the circumstances of his life. The first, anticipated in the late Roman canvases and in part the result of growing technical assurance, was toward a more rapid, spontaneous brushwork, through which the red-brown ground can often be glimpsed, acting as a middle tone. It variously reflects the urgent insecurity of his life, evokes mood and atmosphere, and contributes to pictorial unity.

A second development, to be seen especially in the larger altarpieces (e.g., plate 12 and fig. 4), involved reducing the relative scale of figures in relation to the overall picture space and leaving a substantial gap above their heads. Its effect is to transform the upper part of the painting into an assertive void, which both echoes and absorbs the emotions of the actors. The protagonists are also located back from, rather than breaking through, the picture plane, usually in tightly knit groupings in which they are bound to each other with a minimum of gesture. The combined effect

4. *The Adoration of the Shepherds.* 1609. Oil on canvas, 123⅔ x 83". Museo Regionale, Messina, Sicily

of such strategies is to encourage a more detached and contemplative "reading" of the drama, at arm's length, and a related sense of the fixed and tragic fate of humankind.

Caravaggio's abandonment of all but the most essential gestures is accompanied by a corresponding channeling of feeling into restrained postures and intense facial expressions. The downcast gaze, always a favorite of his but now imbued with a deeper melancholy and pathos, becomes a leitmotif (plates 12–15 and fig. 4). In the Maltese and Sicilian altarpieces it acquires added resonance from the fact that the focus of attention for the onlookers is invariably on or near the ground (e.g., the corpse of Lazarus, and the Christ Child in the Messina *Adoration*). In the Sicilian paintings Caravaggio may have been encouraged in this path of humility by the fact that they were all done for mendicant churches. But he also took advantage of their archetypal subject matter to transform them into more generalized discourses on life and death.

It was the same propensity for harnessing his own increasingly melancholy insights into the human condition to the iconography of Christian art that distinguishes what may have been Caravaggio's two last paintings, a *St. John the Baptist* (Rome, Borghese Gallery) and *David with the Head of Goliath* (plate 15), probably executed for Pope Paul V and his art-loving nephew, Cardinal Scipione Borghese, in the early summer of 1610 as part of a deal whereby Caravaggio was to be pardoned for the murder of Tommasoni and allowed to return to Rome. Recent research suggests that Caravaggio was taking them back with him to Rome when he died at Porto Ercole.

In *David with the Head of Goliath*, the artist offers us a brooding, poetic meditation on his own mortality: The head of Goliath proffered to the viewer by David, who stares down at it with a sad (perhaps valedictory) look, bears the features of Caravaggio himself—ravaged, as one might expect to see them by 1610. It is also a characteristically pungent conceit, with Caravaggio offering up to the Borghese his fictive head instead of the real one that he might have been obliged to forfeit. It is a fitting testament not only to the force of his illusionism but to his long-standing exploration of the interface between sacred imagery and existential reality.

NOTES

1. Interview with Jeremy Isaacs, on BBC 2's "Face to Face" program (1993).

2. For a good summary of Zeri's views and further discussion, see Mina Gregori's catalog entry in *The Age of Caravaggio*, pp. 206–211.

3. Del Monte also owned a version of *The Lute Player*. See Christiansen, 1990 (twice) and Mahon, 1990.

4. The manuscript of Capirola's Lute Book is in the Newberry Library, Chicago. For the translation, see the booklet by Federico Marincola to accompany his CD, *Vincenzo Capirola: Livre de Luth*, Disques Pierre Verany, 1993.

5. For discussion of Caravaggio's technique, see Christiansen, 1986; and Gregori (ed.), 1992.

FURTHER READING

The Age of Caravaggio. Exhibition catalog. New York and Milan: The Metropolitan Museum of Art and Electa International, 1985.

Askew, Pamela. *Caravaggio's "Death of the Virgin."* Princeton, N.J.: Princeton University Press, 1990.

Christiansen, Keith. "Caravaggio and 'L'esempio davanti del naturale.'" *The Art Bulletin* 68, no. 3 (1986), pp. 421–445.

———. *A Caravaggio Rediscovered. "The Lute Player."* New York: The Metropolitan Museum of Art, 1990.

———. "Some Observations on the Relationship Between Caravaggio's Two Treatments of the 'Lute Player.'" *The Burlington Magazine* 1042 (January 1990), pp. 21–26.

Cinotti, Mia. *Michelangelo Merisi detto il Caravaggio: Tutte le Opere* (with a critical essay by Gian Alberto Dell'Acqua). Bergamo: Bolis, 1983.

———. *Caravaggio.* Bergamo: Bolis, 1991.

Cummings, Frederick. "The Meaning of Caravaggio's 'Conversion of the Magdalen.'" *The Burlington Magazine* 859 (October 1974), pp. 572–578.

Enggass, Robert. "La virtù di un vero nobile. L' 'Amore' Giustiniani del Caravaggio." *Palatino* 11 (January–March 1967), pp. 13–20.

Friedlaender, Walter. *Caravaggio Studies.* Princeton, N.J.: Princeton University Press, 1955.

Gash, John. *Caravaggio.* London: Bloomsbury Books, 1988.

———. Review of Pamela Askew: "Caravaggio's 'Death of the Virgin.'" *The Burlington Magazine* 1068 (March 1992), pp. 186–188.

———. "Painting and Sculpture in Early Modern Malta." In *Hospitaller Malta, 1530–1798*, ed. Victor Mallia-Milanes. Msida, Malta: Mireva Publications, 1993, pp. 509–603.

Greaves, James L., and Meryl Johnson. "New Findings on Caravaggio's Technique in the Detroit 'Magdalen.'" *The Burlington Magazine* 859 (October 1974), pp. 564–572.

Gregori, Mina, ed. *Michelangelo Merisi da Caravaggio: Come nascono i Capolavori.* Exhibition catalog. Milan: Electa International, 1992.

Hibbard, Howard. *Caravaggio.* London: Thames and Hudson, 1983.

Jarman, Derek, and Gerald Incandela. *Derek Jarman's "Caravaggio."* London: Thames and Hudson, 1986.

Kitson, Michael. *The Complete Paintings of Caravaggio.* London: Weidenfeld and Nicolson, 1969.

Longhi, Roberto. *Il Caravaggio.* 3rd ed. Rome: Editori Riuniti, 1982.

Mahon, Denis. "Fresh Light on Caravaggio's Earliest Period: His 'Cardsharps' Recovered." *The Burlington Magazine* 1018 (January 1988), pp. 10–25.

———. "The Singing 'Lute Player' by Caravaggio from the Barberini Collection, Painted for Cardinal del Monte." *The Burlington Magazine* 1042 (January 1990), pp. 4–20.

Marini, Maurizio. *Caravaggio. Michelangelo Merisi da Caravaggio "pictor praestantissimus."* Rome: Newton Compton, 1989.

Moir, Alfred. *Caravaggio and His Copyists.* New York: New York University Press, 1976.

———. *Caravaggio.* New York: Harry N. Abrams, 1982.

Nicolson, Benedict. *Caravaggism in Europe.* Turin: Umberto Allemandi, 1989.

Posner, Donald. "Caravaggio's Homo-Erotic Early Works." *The Art Quarterly* 34, no. 3 (1971), pp. 301–324.

Spear, Richard E. *Caravaggio and His Followers.* Exhibition catalog. Rev. ed. New York: Harper and Row, 1975.

First published in 1994 in the United States of America by Rizzoli International Publications, Inc.
300 Park Avenue South
New York, New York 10010

Copyright © 1994 by Rizzoli International Publications, Inc.
Text copyright © 1994 by John Gash

Library of Congress Cataloging-in-Publication Data
Gash, John.
    Caravaggio / by John Gash.
        p. cm. — (Rizzoli art series)
    Includes bibliographical references.
    ISBN 0-8478-1784-9
    1. Caravaggio, Michelangelo Merisi da, 1571–1610—
Criticism and interpretation. I. Title. II. Series.
ND623.C26G33   1994
759.5—dc20   94-16263
                                                  CIP

Designed by Brian Sisco
Series Editor: Norma Broude
Editor: Charles Miers
Assistant Editor: Cathryn Drake
Compositor: Rose Scarpetis

Front cover: see colorplate 3

Printed in Italy

Index to Colorplates

1. *The Rest on the Flight into Egypt.* c. 1595–1596. One of Caravaggio's earliest surviving religious paintings, *The Rest on the Flight* is also the one with the strongest roots in north Italian art. Aspects of its composition, lyrical coloring, and humble, rural piety recall Lotto and Bassano, and Savoldo's *Adoration of the Shepherds.* Its youthful infelicities of design and foreshortening are offset by the equally youthful ardor of Caravaggio's palette and his almost Pre-Raphaelite passion for realistic detail.

2. *The Cardsharps.* c. 1596. This picturesque parable of deceit belonged to Caravaggio's leading early patron in Rome, Cardinal Francesco del Monte. As well as being the most widely copied of Caravaggio's compositions, it exerted a considerable influence on the iconography of the Caravaggist movement, with artists such as Manfredi, Honthorst, Valentin, Régnier, and La Tour concocting ingenious variations upon it.

3. *The Lute Player.* c. 1597–1598. This early example of Caravaggio's penchant for chiaroscuro and "cellar lighting" was painted for his most devoted patron, the Marchese Vincenzo Giustiniani, a keen connoisseur of painting and music. It could have been in connection with it that Caravaggio told Giustiniani that it was as difficult to paint a good picture of flowers as one of figures. The lutenist is singing the madrigal "You Know that I Love You," by the Netherlandish composer Jacob Arcadelt (c. 1514–1568).

4 and 5. *The Calling of St. Matthew* and *The Martyrdom of St. Matthew.* 1599–1600. Caravaggio's first public commission brought him immediate fame. It consisted of two large scenes from the life of St. Matthew, facing each other on opposite walls of the Contarelli chapel, San Luigi dei Francesi. They were commissioned by the Fabbrica of St. Peter's in fulfillment of the will of the French cardinal Matthieu Cointrel (Italianized as Contarelli). In them Caravaggio for the first time fully exploits the tripartite role that he had forged for chiaroscuro: as a means of enhancing the three-dimensionality of forms, as a metaphor for spiritual experience, and as an aid to the articulation of dramatic narrative.

6 and 7. *The Crucifixion of St. Peter* and *The Conversion of St. Paul.* 1601. Caravaggio received a commission from Monsignor Tiberio Cerasi, General Treasurer to Pope Clement VIII, on 24 September 1600, in the wake of his success with the Contarelli laterals, to decorate the side walls of Cerasi's newly acquired chapel in Santa Maria del Popolo with another pair of pictures epitomizing those cornerstones of Counter Reformation ideology: conversion and martyrdom. This time, however, the doctrine of Christian commitment is enshrined in scenes of two separate apostles, Peter and Paul, patron saints of Rome.

8. *The Supper at Emmaus.* 1601. Executed for the nobleman Ciriaco Mattei, into whose palace Caravaggio had moved during the first half of 1601, its mesmeric but ostentatious rhetoric of the real (which includes the basket of fruit teetering implausibly over the edge of the table) is typical of the assertive tone of Caravaggio's naturalism in the first years of his fame.

9. *The Death of the Virgin.* 1601–1602/3. This moving portrayal, painted for the chapel of the canon lawyer Laerzio Cherubini in the Discalced Carmelite church of Santa Maria della Scala, was soon removed from its altar because of its perceived lack of "decorum." Its transgressions were directly related to Caravaggio's polemically naturalistic agenda: the plain, unidealized appearance of the Virgin, whose bloated corpse and deformed feet defy her ecclesiastical status as Queen of Heaven, and the fact that the whole scene too closely resembles an ordinary deathbed situation.

10. *Victorious Cupid.* c. 1603. It may have been in connection with this provocative Cupid for Vincenzo Giustiniani that Caravaggio borrowed a pair of wings from his painter friend Orazio Gentileschi early in 1603. In about 1650, the English painter Richard Symonds was told that Caravaggio's model for Cupid was no other than the future Caravaggist painter known as Cecco del Caravaggio "that was his servant or boy that laid with him."

11. *The Entombment of Christ.* c. 1603–1604. This altarpiece for the newly remodeled chapel of the Pietà belonging to the Vittrice family in the Oratorian church of Santa Maria in Vallicella shows Christ being lowered onto an enormous stone slab placed outside the entrance to the tomb. The outstretched arms of the Virgin (center) and Mary Cleophas (top right) allude, respectively, to the Crucifixion and the Resurrection.

12. *The Raising of Lazarus.* 1609. Caravaggio painted this aptly chosen subject for the chapel of a resident Genoese merchant in Messina, Giovanni Battista de' Lazzari, in the church of the Crucifer fathers. The cross formed by Lazarus's body probably alludes both to the emblem of the Crucifers and to the miracle as a prefiguration of Christ's Crucifixion and Resurrection.

13. *St. John the Baptist.* c. 1606–1610. Caravaggio returned on several occasions to the theme of St. John the Baptist in the wilderness, not least for the opportunity it provided of depicting the young male nude. In keeping with his principle of working directly from life, his St. Johns are always studied afresh from new models—in this case a slightly overweight one.

14. *St. Jerome Writing.* 1607–1608. Caravaggio's St. Johns are paralleled by a comparable group of St. Jeromes. Jerome (c. 340–420) was a hermit whose renowned asceticism appealed to the Counter Reformation mentality. He also translated the Bible into Latin. This rendering of him at work was painted in Malta for Ippolito Malaspina, former admiral of both the papal and Hospitaller fleets, whose arms appear on the right-hand post.

15. *David with the Head of Goliath.* 1610. Caravaggio here presents us with a brooding meditation on his own mortality, completed shortly before his death: The head of Goliath proffered to the viewer by David bears the artist's own features.

1. *The Rest on the Flight into Egypt.* c. 1595–1596. Oil on canvas, 51 x 63". Galleria Doria-Pamphilj, Rome. Photograph courtesy Scala/Art Resource, New York

2. *The Cardsharps.* c. 1596. Oil on canvas, 37¹/₁₆ x 51⁹/₁₆".
Kimbell Art Museum, Fort Worth, Texas

3. *The Lute Player.* c. 1597–1598. Oil on canvas, 37 x 47". Hermitage Museum, St. Petersburg. Photograph courtesy Scala/Art Resource, New York

4. The Calling of St. Matthew. 1599–1600. Oil on canvas, 127 x 134".
Contarelli Chapel, San Luigi dei Francesi, Rome. Photograph courtesy
Scala/Art Resource, New York

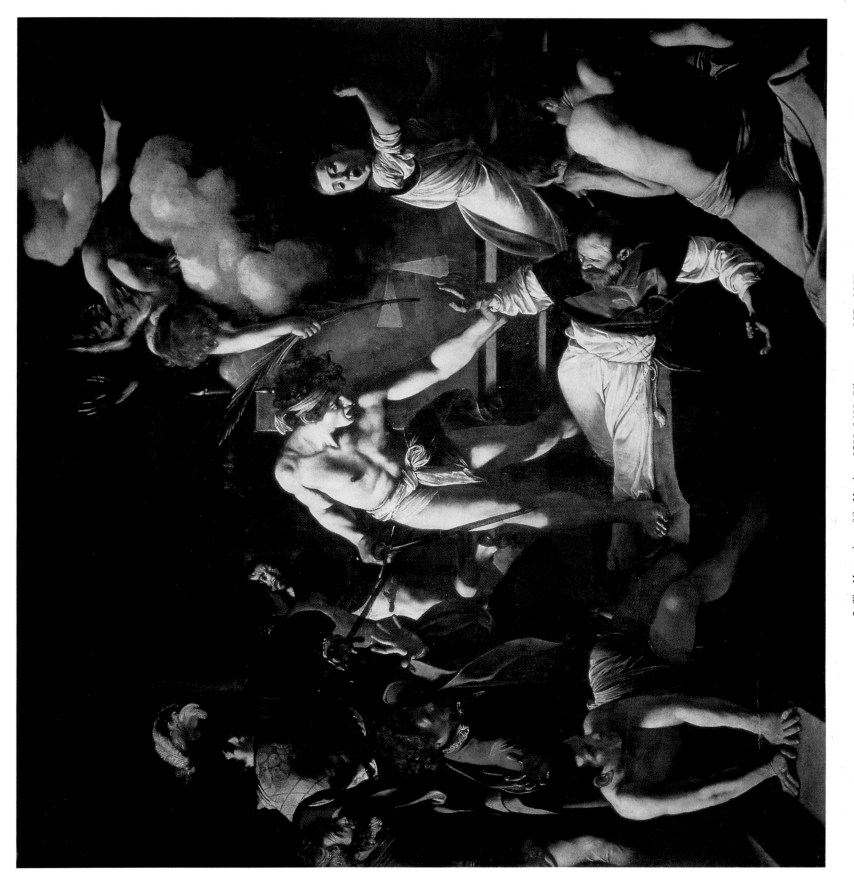

5. *The Martyrdom of St. Matthew.* 1599–1600. Oil on canvas, 127 x 135".
Contarelli Chapel, San Luigi dei Francesi, Rome. Photograph courtesy
Scala/Art Resource, New York

6. *The Crucifixion of St. Peter.* 1601. Oil on canvas, 90½ x 69". Cerasi Chapel, Santa
Maria del Popolo, Rome. Photograph courtesy Scala/Art Resource, New York

7. *The Conversion of St. Paul*. 1601. Oil on canvas, 90½ x 69". Cerasi Chapel, Santa
Maria del Popolo, Rome. Photograph courtesy Scala/Art Resource, New York

8. *The Supper at Emmaus.* 1601. Oil on canvas, 54½ x 77". The National Gallery,
London

9. *The Death of the Virgin.* 1601–1602/3. Oil on canvas, 145 x 96½". Musée
du Louvre, Paris

10. *Victorious Cupid.* c. 1603. Oil on canvas, 60½ x 43". Staatliche Museen, Gemäldegalerie, Berlin. Courtesy of Bildarchiv Preussischer Kulturbesitz, Berlin. Photograph by Jorg Anders

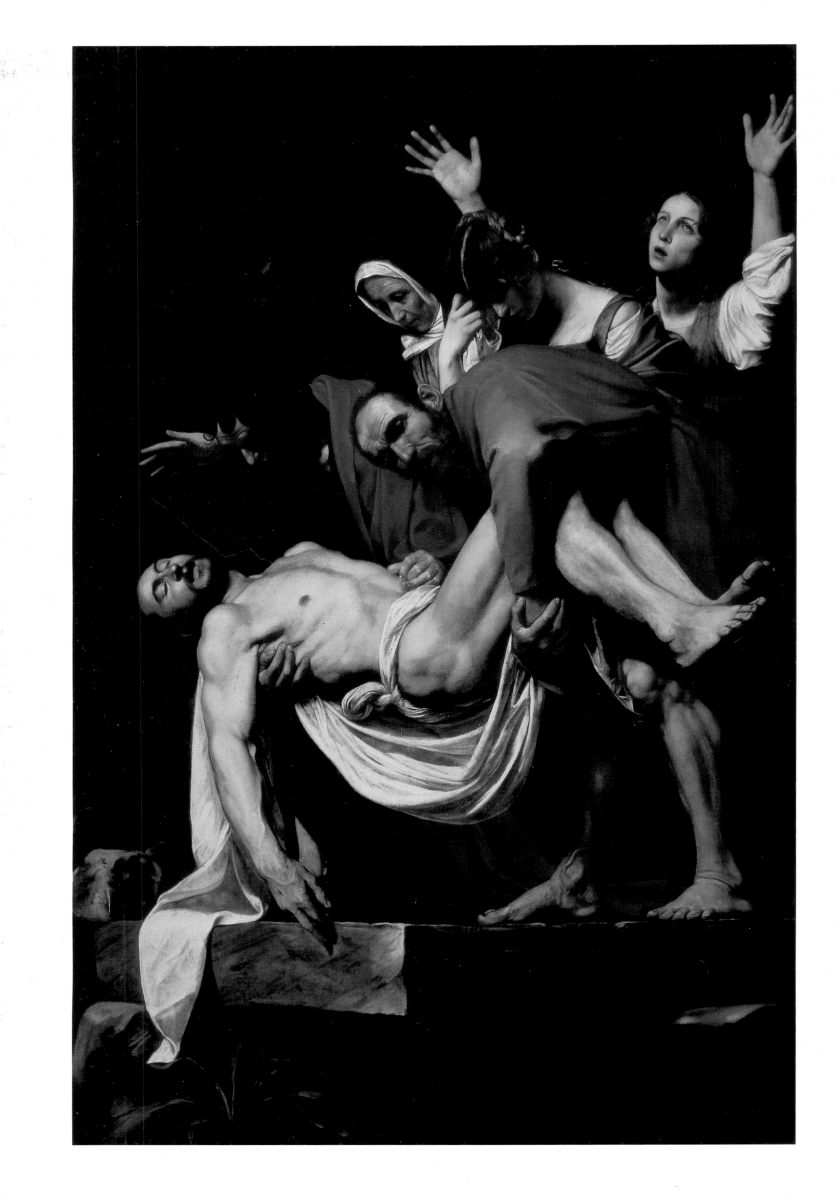

11. *The Entombment of Christ.* c. 1603–1604. Oil on canvas, 118 x 80".
Pinacoteca Vaticana, Rome. Photograph by M. Sarri

12. *The Raising of Lazarus.* 1609. Oil on canvas, 149½ x 108". Museo Regionale,
Messina, Sicily. Photograph courtesy Scala/Art Resource, New York

13. *St. John the Baptist.* c. 1606–1610. Oil on canvas, 39 x 53". Galleria Nazionale d'Arte Antica, Rome. Photograph courtesy Scala/Art Resource, New York

14. *St. Jerome Writing.* 1607–1608. Oil on canvas, 46 x 62". Co-Cathedral of St. John, Valletta. Photograph courtesy Scala/Art Resource, New York

15. *David with the Head of Goliath*. 1610. Oil on canvas, 49 x 39½".
Borghese Gallery, Rome. Photograph courtesy Scala/Art Resource, New York